Sabrina Zabel

Role-breaking and role-remaking in Angela Carter's "The Bloody Chamber"

GRIN - Verlag für akademische Texte

Der GRIN Verlag mit Sitz in München hat sich seit der Gründung im Jahr 1998 auf die Veröffentlichung akademischer Texte spezialisiert.

Die Verlagswebseite www.grin.com ist für Studenten, Hochschullehrer und andere Akademiker die ideale Plattform, ihre Fachtexte, Studienarbeiten, Abschlussarbeiten oder Dissertationen einem breiten Publikum zu präsentieren.

Dokument Nr. V135158 aus dem GRIN Verlagsprogramm

Sabrina Zabel

Role-breaking and role-remaking in Angela Carter's "The Bloody Chamber"

GRIN Verlag

Bibliografische Information der Deutschen Nationalbibliothek: Die Deutsche Bibliothek verzeichnet diese Publikation in der Deutschen Nationalbibliografie; detaillierte bibliografische Daten sind im Internet über http://dnb.d-nb.de/ abrufbar.

1. Auflage 2008
Copyright © 2008 GRIN Verlag
http://www.grin.com/
Druck und Bindung: Books on Demand GmbH, Norderstedt Germany
ISBN 978-3-640-42480-1

Otto – von – Guericke – Universität Magdeburg

Fakultät für Geistes-, Sozial- und Erziehungswissenschaften

Institut für fremdsprachliche Philologien

Seminar:
Gothic Fiction
SS 2007

role-breaking and role-remaking

in Angela Carter's

The Bloody Chamber

Sabrina Zabel
6. Semester LG Anglistik/Germanistik

Magdeburg, 2008-01-31

Content

1. Introduction

> The attainment of female subjectivity in spite of female sexual maturation, the oppression of female sexuality, the passive role of females bound in the confines of marriage, and as accumulated property are some of the issues that Carter addresses in The Bloody Chamber within the framework of the fairytale genre.[1]

Angela Carter adopts Perrault's fairy-tale *Bluebeard* in her story *The Bloody Chamber* and transfers it into a feminist rewriting. She breaks through the prescribed role-understanding of women and men in society.

Society defines women as being passive, men as being active in every domain of the everyday life. Angela Carter draws a picture against this stigmatization. She does not define women as being merely subversive; victims of male authority and simply fulfilling their role. She wants to show that women have the ability to gain independence and a free will by giving male qualities to her female characters or letting them not behave like society expects them to behave.

In society men are said to be powerful and oppressing their wives. They show true qualities of masculinity and exploit their wife's innocence and naivety. Carter on the one hand portrays men as embodying this prescribed role, but also adds female qualities to their actions and behaviours, or being overpowered by their female counterparts.

This paper shall show in how far Angela Carter adapts constructed role models, changes them or invents new ones.

Therefore the paper is divided into two sections: The first gives a brief overview about the time period as this text is written against the background of the gothic era. The second part concentrates on *The Bloody Chamber*, which is first of all based on Perrault's Bluebeard story - to realize the differences to the original and understand their functions with the help of the before described background knowledge. Afterwards, an analysis of each character in the story should make clear the concept of Carter's role-breaking and role-remaking.

---

[1] <http://www.megaessays.com/viewpaper/12503.html> (16/07/2007).

2. Female gothic writers and female characters

"Themes such as the suppression of female desires, females being objectified, confined to a domestic life are all critically challenged in this expose of society then and today."[2] The man is always portrayed as being the bread-winner, powerful, intelligent, whereas the woman is mostly connected with domestic tasks. Because of this general understanding women are more likely presented as being suppressed, victimized and passive in female literature, including gothic female literature. Female writers construct themselves as being oppressed by men, like men present themselves as manipulating, aggressive forces who want their wives to obey them.[3] Women wanted to express the feelings and fears they experience in a relationship, but could not reveal in public. Therefore they chose the written form to communicate with other women and encourage them.

The gothic novel makes use of this cliché in that it assumes women's passive and suppressed role within society, but adds the female will in order to destroy the masculine public world.

> [...] the female gothic novel represented women who ostensibly appear to be conforming to their acceptable roles within the patriarchy but who actually subvert the father's power at every possible occasion and them retreat to studied postures of conformity whenever they risk exposure to public censure.[4]

On the one hand women are depicted as being imprisoned by their husbands or male counterparts; on the other hand they gain power over them by their spiritual strength.

---

[2] <http://www.dooyoo.co.uk/printed-books/the-bloody-chamber-angela-carter/1024374/> (16/07/2007).
[3] c.f. Hoeveler, Diana Long: *Gothic Feminism. The Professionalization of Gender from Charlotte Smith to the Brontës*. Pennsylvania: The Pennsylvania State University Press 1998. p. 4.
[4] ibid. p. 6.

> Women are always represented as persecuted, deprived of power, and imprisoned, yet the places which confine them often protect them too. The heroine escapes from imprisonment into a natural world that symbolizes her own free nature, the spiritual freedom which she always maintains under physical oppression.[5]

Women create a fantasy world in which they escape their internment and oppression by their husbands and experience their own self. In this imaginative world they are not weak; they do not just accept and survive. Women's situation is not seen as their destiny; they are not defined through their male partners. In the typical gothic novel the female character struggles against patriarchy. This struggle is of an ideological nature because it takes place between reality and desire in a sexual, psychic, economic, political, social or religious field: Reality symbolizes the power within the political society, whereas desire constitutes the individual urge. Female gothic writers fictively redefine sexuality, family, patrimonialism and patrilineality they are unable to experience in everyday life.

In general the gothic novel pictures the woman as a heroine who is able to obliterate patriarchy because she outsmarts her male oppressive opponent.[6]

3. Angela Carter's *The Bloody Chamber*

3.1 Charles Perrault's *Bluebeard* as literary source

The Bluebeard story was created by the French writer Charles Perrault. It was first published in 1697 in his collection *Histoires ou contes du temps passé (Stories or Tales of Past Times)* and intended to be written as a fairy-tale for adult readers.[7]

A wealthy man named Bluebeard is living on his own in his splendid house and still is searching for a woman to marry him. He had had several women before who always ran away from him because of his physical disfigurement: "a blue beard, which made him look so frightfully ugly that the first impulse of every

---

[5] Spencer, Jane: *The Rise of the Woman Novelist. From Aphra Behn to Jane Austen.* Oxford: Blackwell Publishers 1986. p.194.

[6] c.f. Hoeveler, Diana Long: *Gothic Feminism. The Professionalization of Gender from Charlotte Smith to the Brontës.* p. 6-19.

[7] c.f. <http://www.endicott-studio.com/rdrm/forblue3.html> (16/07/2007).

woman and girl he met was to run away from him."[8] He wishes to marry one of the lady's daughters who live in the same place, but none of them can hide their dislike towards him. Therefore he invites the three women and their friends to stay at his house for one week and hopes to convince at least one of the daughters of his qualities. Fatima, the younger daughter, quickly recognizes that Bluebeard's beard does not make him that ugly as she supposed. She is delightfully impressed by his kindness and does not hesitate to accept his proposal.

After their marriage, he has to leave her alone because of a journey for at least six weeks. He leaves her a bundle of keys to each room in the house and at the same time forbids her to make use of the small one of polished steel, which belongs to a little room at the end of the corridor. After he left her, her curiosity defeats her husband's prohibit. She enters the room and comes across the dead bodies of his former wives. Being completely horrified she loses the key which falls onto the bloody ground. She is not able to wipe the blood off and hides the key. Bluebeard returns earlier from his journey and at first asks for the keys he had given to her. Still shaking and terrified she hands him the bundle, hoping that he does not recognize that the key to the forbidden chamber is missing. He notices the loss of the key and after calling upon her to fetch the key, realizes its bloody spot. She disobeyed his command and now has to join his former wives in the forbidden chamber. Bluebeard allows her to say her last prayers before he is going to kill her. She prays that her brothers shall come to rescue her. Fortunately her prayers are answered and one of her brothers kills Bluebeard with his sword.

Perrault's Bluebeard story can be described as "a gruesome cautionary tale about the dangers of marriage (on the one hand) and the perils of greed and curiosity (on the other)".[9] In the beginning of the story the husband is represented as being kind, generous and betrayed by his wives because they disobey his commands. In the end he is depicted as being evil, a monster, who is willing to kill his own wife cruelly. Perrault includes two morals in his story, rather casting a positive light on the husband than feeling sympathy for the female counterpart. He

---

[8] <http://www.kellscraft.com/bluebeard/bluebeard01.html> (10/01/2007).
[9] <http://www.endicott-studio.com/rdrm/forblue3.html> (16/07/2007).

emphasizes that the female curiosity in this marriage is a form of transgression and that the husband just acts in response to the provocative actions of his wife.

The topic of disobedience in Perrault's work was liked to be reprinted and recounted by several writers until it was expanded in the nineteenth and twentieth century. Some authors were of the opinion that Bluebeard's wife's disobedience is sexual in nature and that therefore "the blood–stained key symboliz[es] the act of infidelity."[10] The psychologist Bruno Bettlheim sees the Bluebeard story as "'a cautionary tale which warns: Women, don't give in to your sexual curiosity; men, don't permit yourself to be carried away by your anger at being sexually betrayed.'"[11] In contradiction, the novelist Lydia Millet states that the husband is in charge because he left his wife the key to the forbidden chamber while going on a trip.[12]

3.2 *Bluebeard's* processing in *The Bloody Chamber*

Angela Carter translated Charles Perrault's fairy-tales in 1977. She was so much fascinated by the literary genre that she herself published a collection of stories in 1979 which retell the classical fairy-tales.[13] This collection is titled the *The Bloody Chamber* and can not be seen as a mere rewriting of traditional fairy-tales. The stories are interconnected, whereas every story depicts a certain theme which is represented in another story before and "'comments on a different aspect of it.'"[14] The blood is the element which binds all tales together.

The title story *The Bloody Chamber* textually concentrates on the Bluebeard story written by Charles Perrault in the seventeenth century. Its contents are similar except that Angela Carter replaces the appearance of the brothers with the coincidental rescue by the heroine's mother. Carter depicts her as the central

---

[10] <http://www.endicott-studio.com/rdrm/forblue3.html> (16/07/2007).
[11] ibid.
[12] c.f. <http://www.endicott-studio.com/rdrm/forblue3.html> (16/07/2007).
[13] c.f. Makinen, Merja: "Angela Carter's The Bloody Chamber and the Decolonization of Feminine Sexuality". In: *Feminist Review* 42 (autumn 1992):. p. 3.
[14] Gamble, Sarah: *Angela Carter. Writing from the frontline.* Edinburgh: Edinburgh University Press 1997. p. 132.

figure in the story and attributes man-like qualities to her. Whereas in the Bluebeard story she is portrayed as lady-like and just being the mother of two daughters.

In Perrault's story the two brothers are presented as the quintessence of masculinity: the one appearing as a dragoon, the other as a musketeer. Carter decreases the power of male characters in *The Bloody Chamber* by adding a weak piano-tuner as a secondary male figure. He is engaged by the husband to tune the piano so that his wife can play when she likes to do so. This character is blind and stands in contrast to the husband's powerful and aggressive appearance.

"Like Perrault, however, Carter has also included a coda: Beware of men, beware of becoming subservient to men."[15] Although she adopts Perrault's Bluebeard story, she redefines it by using strong female characters and feministic attitudes. "Her aim was to uncover the unconscious patriarchal themes repeatedly found in folklores and fairytales, and to subvert these in order to shed light on the post-feminist perspective."[16] The husband, as in the Bluebeard story, is not presented as being solely handsome and good anymore. He is rather seen as the evil force, victimizing his wife. But nonetheless he is unable to overpower another character, a female personality: his wife's mother.

Besides Angela Carter's interest in fairy-tales, she preferred the literary genre because

> the form's innate flexibility thus allows it to illuminate experiences embedded in social and material conditions … [and] reveal … how human behaviour is embedded in material circumstances, in the laws of dowry, land tenure, feudal obedience, domestic hierarchies and material dispositions, and that when these pass and change, behaviour may change with them.[17]

Likewise she confirms that this genre is connected with women who were both tellers and writers and therefore responsible for its development.

---

[15]<http://www.engl.niu.edu/kwezner/Spring%2005%20Engl%20110/Angela%20Carter%20biograph y.doc> (16/7/2007).

[16] <http://www.dooyoo.co.uk/printed-books/the-bloody-chamber-angela-carter/1024374/> (16/7/07).

[17] Gamble, Sarah: Angela Carter. *Writing from the frontline.* p. 130.

Even though fairy-tales are regarded as fantastic miraculous narratives predominantly written for children, Angela Carter wants to show that there is more behind it than darkness and magic: She wants to extract the uncanny latent content of the traditional fairy-tale. She constitutes another image of the traditionally known fairy-tale by changing the cosy atmosphere into a "fierce, dark, erotic, gothic and [...] dripping with gore"[18] one.

3.3 Role-reversal in *The Bloody Chamber*

Since Angela Carter is a feminist gothic writer, she apparently adopts the male and female role's which are presented in every gothic novel, as well as in society. On the first sight the husband is aggressive, powerful and oppressing his wife. Likewise his wife is weak, intimidated and dependent on her husband. But *The Bloody Chamber* is more than a mere gothic novel, because Angela Carter does not just concentrate on stereotypical elements of this era. She adds new qualities to the characters which break through the previously described understanding and construction. Besides she invents other figures which indicate a role reversal.

> Carter transforms the tale of Bluebeard into a feminist story in her version entitled "The Bloody Chamber" by placing the mother in the role of savior, allowing the protagonist to participate in her own rescue, and subtracting strength from the secondary male figures.[19]

The Bloody Chamber is a first person narrative, in which Angela Carter does not give a name to any character, except the piano-tuner. There is no specific time, no specific place mentioned; there are just hints given.

---

[18] Gamble, Sarah: *Angela Carter. Writing from the frontline.* p. 132.
[19] <http://www.gradesaver.com/classicnotes/titles/bloodychamber/essay1.html> (16/7/07).

3.3.1 The two main characters in their marriage

3.3.1.1 The ostensibly innocent protagonist

The female protagonist in *The Bloody Chamber* leaves her hometown Paris because she marries a wealthy man who wants to live with her in his castle. She is depicted as detaching from her mother, driving "away from girlhood, away from the white enclosed quietude of [her] mother's apartment, into the unguessable country of marriage."[20] She likes to leave her past behind and begin a new step in her live, but at the same time recognizes "a pang of loss as if, when [her husband] puts the gold band on [her] finger, [she] had [...] ceased to be her [mother's] child in becoming his wife."[21] This situation is common in every day's society as well, as the marriage is seen as freedom from the family's home, in that context the maternal home.

The narrator states that she truly loves her husband and wants to share her life with him, but does not know where it would take her. She knows that she has to obey him like society prescribes to every female in a relationship. She sightlessly accepts her circumstances due to her love for her husband, although she, at the same time, feels unwell about the unknown when they arrive at the "never-to-be-visited station"[22]:

> [...] all the paraphernalia of the everyday world from which I, with my stunning marriage, had exiled myself. Into marriage, into exile; I sensed it, I knew it [...] I would always be alone [...] all had conspired to seduce me so utterly that I could not say I felt one single twinge of regret for the world of tartines and maman that now receded from me as if drawn away on a string [...][23]

The heroine is lost in thought about a warm and hearty relationship and at the same time perceives the misty, dark landscape and the cold, empty inside of the castle which does not appear threatening to her.

---

[20] Carter, Angela: The Bloody Chamber. In: *Burning your Boats. Collected Short Stories*. London: Vintage 1996. p. 111.
[21] ibid.
[22] ibid. p. 115.
[23] ibid.

What looks like the portraying of an innocent, intimidated and shy girl drawn into the new life as wife, in reality is an illustration of an alternative evil competing with the masculine evil presented by the husband.[24]

> His wedding gift, clasped round my throat. A choker of rubies, two inches wide, like an extraordinary precious slit throat. [...] I caught sight of myself in the mirror. And I saw myself, suddenly, as he saw me, my pale face, the way the muscles in my neck stuck out like thin wire. I saw how much that cruel necklace became me. And, for the first time in my innocent and confined life, I sensed in myself a potentiality for corruption that took my breath away.[25]

This contrary perception and adaptation emphasizes what Carter wants to establish: "[...] she stresses the relationship between women's subjective sexuality and their objective role as property: young girls get bought by wealth, one way or another."[26] The protagonist is isolated because she is living in this castle surrounded by nothing lively, but expects sexual initiation.

While her husband is on a business trip, she feels left alone and bored to death. She is angry with him about leaving her alone. She calls her mother, but even this telephone call does not prevent her innermost feelings of loneliness.

> Within these Gothic realms the individual is powerless because isolated; here, everything can happen and, more importantly, from these cages nobody can flee. [...]The loneliness enforced on the individual – here in absolute isolation – creates an insurmountable sense of disempowerment which is stiflingly terrorising.[27]

She comes across the bunch of keys he left her and the curiosity to have a look into each room rises in her. She wants to know everything about her husband, his preferences, and his character.

---

[24] c.f. <http://www.wickedness.net/Evil/Evil%208/ozum%20paper.pdf> (16/7/07) p. 3.

[25] Carter, Angela: The Bloody Chamber. In: Burning your Boats. Collected Short Stories. pp. 114.

[26] Makinen, Merja: "Angela Carter's The Bloody Chamber and the Decolonization of Feminine Sexuality". In: Feminist Review 42. p. 10.

[27] Carter, Angela: Identity Constructed/Deconstructed. Heidelberg: Universitätsverlag C. Winter 1997. p. 41.

The gothic heroine's goal throughout most of the text is to ascertain the "secret" that the patriarchy has managed to keep from her, either through an elaborate system of walls and locked rooms (the prison and asylum) or through the power of language to dissemble, to reveal and conceal at the same time (missing marriage licence or wills).[28]

In Angela Carter's story the female protagonist wants to find out about the secret that lies behind the wall in a locked room to primarily learn more about her husband's soul. She does not symbolize the

image of the female which is mostly associated with the good, the decent, the innocent and naïve in most of the traditional fairy-tales [...] [she] is rendered either to have inclinations towards pervert sexual practices or to be violently harmful for the opposite sex.[29]

In this sense one might argue that the second is not primarily applicable for *The Bloody Chamber*. Her husband would not have given the bundles of keys to her if he had known that her curiosity would outsmart herself. He wanted her to find his dead wives in the bloody chamber; otherwise he would not have left the key at home in charge of her. She wants to experience sexual arousal and is interested in pervert sexual practices, as well. This is obvious when he strips her in their wedding night: "He in his London tailoring; she, bare as a lamp chop. Most pornographic off all confrontations. And so my purchaser unwrapped his bargain. And, as at the opera, when I had first seen my flesh in his eyes, I was aghast to feel myself stirring."[30] The protagonist is involved in the pervert and pornographic world of her husband. Later on she finds pornographic books in her husband's library and by browsing through them admits: "I knew enough for what I saw in that book to make me gasp."[31] However in this sense it is more than just the sexual arousal which was mentioned before.

---

[28] Hoeveler, Diana Long: Gothic Feminism. The Professionalization of Gender from Charlotte Smith to the Brontës. pp. 21.

[29] <http://www.wickedness.net/Evil/Evil%208/ozum%20paper.pdf> (16/7/07) p. 1.

[30] Carter, Angela: The Bloody Chamber. In: *Burning your Boats. Collected Short Stories.* p. 119.

[31] ibid. p. 120.

Carter

> [...] deconstruct[s] and demystif[ies] evil which is closely linked
> with masculinity and patriarchal values and norms and that the
> storie[...] intentionally display[s] a potential harshness of the
> female evil simultaneously existing with the masculine evil. This
> attachment of the evil to the feminine attributions is in fact to
> foreground the female body and voice which can at times be as
> lustful, self-conscious, vulgar, reckless, harsh and independent
> as the body and the voice of a male.[32]

The young woman confesses that

> [...] [she] was not afraid of him, but of [her]self. [She] seemed
> reborn in his unreflective eyes, reborn in unfamiliar shapes.
> [She] hardly recognised [her]self from his descriptions of [her]
> and yet ... [she] blushed again, unnoticed, to think he might
> have chosen [her] because, in [her] innocence, he sensed a rare
> talent for corruption.[33]

The protagonist admits her please for the sexual encounters throughout the novel
until she discovers the bloody chambers with her husband's former dead wives in
it. From then on she removes her consent. The reader begins to doubt her
innocence and ignorance more than before which is stressed by the fact that she
disobeyed his demand to not use the small key to his chamber. Her curiosity
overpowers his prohibition because she wants to disclose his secret. This action
can be understood as the first stage of getting her way. She is not fearful; she
does not fulfil the role, the identity society imposes on her.

Meanwhile her husband is on a business trip and leaves her alone with the
piano-tuner and his employees. Still feeling lonely, bored and angry about him
leaving her alone, she now wants to call her mother again and tell her about the
horrifying observations. Unfortunately the line is dead and she from then on feels
more drawn into a hopeless situation. Now the castle completely functions as a
symbol of trap of this woman and the outside natural world as the female freedom
she is not able to gain anymore.[34]

---

[32] <http://www.wickedness.net/Evil/Evil%208/ozum%20paper.pdf> (16/7/07) p. 2.
[33] Carter, Angela: The Bloody Chamber. In: Burning your Boats. Collected Short Stories. p. 124.
[34] c.f. Spencer, Jane: The Rise of the Woman Novelist. From Aphra Behn to Jane Austen. p. 194.

"Her precarious safety lies in her innocence [...]"[35], but when she does not take his orders and discovers the bloody chamber, she loses it. This is symbolized by her husband leaving her "not only with a blood-red ruby necklace, [...] but with a blood-red brand on her forehead; [...]".[36] She can only be reborn and purified through her mother's rescue, or she is her husband's next victim of his perverse fantasy. The mark on her forehead is the manifestation of her curiosity and her inclination for corruption. She is glad that the piano-tuner as her new lover can not see it because of his blindness. "No paint nor powder, no matter how thick or white, can mask that red mark on my forehead; I am glad he cannot see it – not for fear of his revulsion, since I know he sees me clearly with his heart – but, because it spares my shame."[37]

3.3.1.2 The evil husband

The husband is depicted as being evil and violating his wives "[...] captured within the construction of masculinity."[38] He likes to kill his wives to live out his perverse fantasies. He possesses a collection of pornographic books and describes them as being his "prayerbooks".[39]

Being interested in the philosophy of de Sade and Bataille in terms of sexuality, Carter processes these elements in *The Bloody Chamber* and makes him appear as the last Sadeian monster. "[The] monster's bride is thin, pale and virginal, exactly the kind of protected maiden de Sade delights in having his evil folk ravish, humiliate and kill."[40] His bloody chamber "represents the deepest, darkest realm of the Sadeian erotic fantasy"[41], "a room designed for desecration and some dark night of unimaginable lovers whose embraces were annihilation."[42]

---

[35] Gamble, Sarah: *Angela Carter. Writing from the frontline.* p. 154.
[36] Atwood, Margaret: "Running with the Tiger". In: Lorna Sage (ed.): *Flesh and Mirror.* London: Vigaro 1995. pp. 123.
[37] Carter, Angela: The Bloody Chamber. In: *Burning your Boats. Collected Short Stories.* p. 143.
[38] Makinen, Merja: "Angela Carter's The Bloody Chamber and the Decolonization of Feminine Sexuality". In: *Feminist Review* 42. p. 13.
[39] Carter, Angela: The Bloody Chamber. In: *Burning your Boats. Collected Short Stories.* p. 120.
[40] Atwood, Margaret: "Running with the Tiger". In: Lorna Sage (ed.): *Flesh and Mirror.* p. 123.
[41] Gamble, Sarah: *Angela Carter. Writing from the frontline.* 154.
[42] Carter, Angela: The Bloody Chamber. In: *Burning your Boats. Collected Short Stories.* p. 131.

His appearance is described as a "dark, leonine shape of his head and [...] the opulent male scent of leather and spices [...] accompanied him."[43] Carter portrays him as a tiger, a carnivore, which is addicted to meat. The motif of meat signifies objectification: the relationship of sensation to an object. The object in this sense is his wife. The motif of meat is interrelated with that of flesh. Flesh symbolizes pleasure. He says:

> Don't loiter, girl! Do you think I shall lose appetite for the meal if you are so long about serving it? No; I shall grow hungrier, more ravenous with each moment, more cruel...Run to me, run! I have a place prepared for your exquisite corpse in my display of flesh![44]

In the beginning of the story his wife is the victim of his desire. In the end he becomes the victim of his wife's mother, who enters the story in person to rescue her daughter. That's why "The puppet master, open-mouthed, wide eyed, impotent at the last, saw his dolls break free of their strings, abandon the rituals he had ordained for them since time began and start to live for themselves."[45]

3.3.1.2.1 Function of mirrors and the male gaze

The bedroom in which the couple wants to spend its wedding night is decorated with mirrors. These mirrors function as metaphorical elements helping to identify oneself. The protagonist sees herself being surrounded by a dozen of husbands, whereas the husband creates his own harem of women by hanging up these mirrors. There is the idea that society or the outside world imposes an image on a person which the person adopts mimetically and consequently losing identity by doing so.[46] By looking in the mirror the protagonist identifies herself as being entangled in a web of power - her husband. She loses a part of her identity because she becomes the object of his desire, has fear and feels insecure. He is lecherous, she is anxious: "[...] the child with her sticklike limbs, naked but for her

---

[43] ibid p. 112.
[44] ibid p. 141.
[45] Carter, Angela: The Bloody Chamber. In: *Burning your Boats. Collected Short Stories.* p. 142.
[46] c.f. Carter, Angela: *Identity Constructed/Deconstructed.* p. 43.

button boots, her gloves, shielding her face with her hand as though her face were the last repository of her modesty; and the old monocled lecher who examined her, limb by limb."[47] She is drawn into being an object rather assuming an active subjectivity. This active-passive binary is even common in our society today as we mostly associate men with gazing at women and women being the ones who are gaped at. She is looked at and disempowered by him starring at her. The mirror and the looking-glass both function as symbols of the male gaze:

> [...] [T]he mirror becomes symbolic of the power of the male gaze, the voyeuristic stare of pornography, the impersonal gaze behind peep-show slots; it is, indeed, 'the eye of power' (M. Foucault) under whose influence women are turned into passive objects of male desire, respectlessly stared at and confronted with the power embodied in the anonymous eye.[48]

This is even emphasized by her feelings of being observed in the train:

> I heard no change in his breathing but my heightened excited senses told me that he was awake and gazing at me. A huge man, an enormous man, and his eyes, dark and motionless as those eyes the ancient Egyptians painted upon their sarcophagi, fixed upon me. I felt a certain tension in the pit of my stomach, to be so watched in such silence.[49]

The protagonist "[...] appears defenceless, even unable and unwilling to gather the strength to act: the living woman has become a living image out of a book of erotic art, a static 'tableau vivant' proposed to her by her husband."[50] She becomes his commodity, his property utilized when he needs her.

3.3.1.3 The mother as the saviour

The mother is the central figure in The Bloody Chamber. Her appearance points out that Angela Carter does not stick to fixed roles. She does not present her as

---

[47] Carter, Angela: The Bloody Chamber. In: Burning your Boats. Collected Short Stories. p. 119.
[48] Carter, Angela: Identity Constructed/Deconstructed. p. 48.
[49] Carter, Angela: The Bloody Chamber. In: Burning your Boats. Collected Short Stories. p. 116.
[50] Carter, Angela: Identity Constructed/Deconstructed. p. 48.

passive or powerless, as women are supposed to be. The mother has a rather unfeminine history and is looked up by her daughter for her man-like abilities.[51]

> My eagle-featured indomitable mother; what other student at the Conservatoire could boast that her mother had outfaced a junkful of Chinese pirates; nursed a village through a visitation of the plague, shot a man-eating tiger with her own hand [...][52]

The protagonist is proud of her mother's qualities who is introduced as a tiger-shooter and tough-minded. This introduction of the mother "breaks up the victor/victim tableau in Bluebeard's castle courtyard, it introduces a wild-card third element into the fixed dualism of the couple."[53] The invention of the mother states that certain characters need not be either female or male; representing their prescribed roles within the social frame. The mother is the example for moving between two poles: being female, but at the same time having qualities men are mostly associated with.

Mother and daughter have an intimidated relationship what is expressed by their telephone call while the husband is on his trip. The protagonist actually wants to call her mother in a dead waste of time but can not wait any longer because she feels so dreadfully alone. She does not tell her mother about her lonesomeness; she wants to make her believe that the decision to marry him was what she really wanted and wished. She wants to express the strength and bravery her mother had exemplified to her through her own life, but bursts into tears when she hears her voice. She lies that she is weeping about the gold bath taps she has got in her bathroom.

This situation causes the mother to come to visit her daughter. Knowing her daughter well enough, she had never heard her daughter cry before. The husband is just preparing to chop his wife's head off, as the mother suddenly enters the castle and "without a moment's hesitation, she raised [the protagonist's] father's gun, took aim and put a single, irreproachable bullet through [the] husband's

---

[51] c.f. <http://www.gradesaver.com/classicnotes/titles/bloodychamber/essay1.html> (16/7/07).
[52] Carter, Angela: The Bloody Chamber. In: Burning your Boats. Collected Short Stories. p. 111.
[53] Gamble, Sarah: Angela Carter. Writing from the frontline. p. 155.

head."[54] She has a redemptive role because she rescues her daughter from her husband's imprisonment and prevents her from becoming one of his dead wives.

3.3.1.4 The feminized piano-tuner

The piano-tuner is the weak male character in the story who does not represent power which is associated with men in general. He is also the only character who has a name: Jean-Yves. He is engaged by the husband to tune the piano so that his wife can play while he is away on his journey. The protagonist and the piano-tuner share the music as their hobby, while his job is to tune the piano and her hobby to play it. She allows him to listen to her while she is playing.

He is blind, which also can be seen as a sign for his weakened power because he can not see and might not recognize everything that happens around him. His interest in music can as well be interpreted as an element of weakness, because mostly men are just living for their business like the protagonist' husband does.

After the protagonist investigated the bloody chamber she goes into the music room trying to forget about the horrifying experience:

> [...] perhaps I thought my own particular magic might help me, now, that I could create a pentacle out of music that would keep me from harm for, if my music had first ensnared him, might it not also give me the power to free myself from him?[55]

Somebody is knocking on the door and she feels relieved that she "[...] saw, not the massive irredeemable bulk of [her] husband but the slight, stooping figure of the piano-tuner [...]."[56] He heard her walking up and down in her room, thinking that she might not be able to sleep and stumbled over the bundle of keys. He does not behave in the way the protagonist's husband does as he makes compliments about her way of playing certain pieces of music. She is flattered by his statements

---

[54] Carter, Angela: The Bloody Chamber. In: *Burning your Boats. Collected Short Stories.* p. 142.
[55] Carter, Angela: The Bloody Chamber. In: *Burning your Boats. Collected Short Stories.* p. 133.
[56] ibid p. 134.

and in him finds a new companion; a companion who takes her like she is and appreciates what she does.

> When I heard you play this afternoon, I thought I'd never heard such a touch. Such technique. A treat for me, to hear a virtuoso! So I crept up to your door now, humbly as a little dog might, madame, and put my ear to the keyhole and listened, and listened [...].[57]

He functions as the counterpart of the husband because he does not depict the established male behaviour. He can not be associated with elements of violence and abuse against women. He is perceptive, sympathetic and recognizes her suffering because he says: "You are in some great distress [...] no bride should suffer so much, so early in her marriage."[58] He inspires confidence which leads the protagonist to read the piano-tuner in her dreadful observations in the bloody chamber.

In contrast to the husband representing pure masculinity, the piano-tuner is feminized, being malleable in his words and his outward appearance.[59] As the protagonist, he appears to be lamb-like, sweet, in contrast to the husband's tiger-like entry.

This femininity becomes even more obvious when the husband returns from his trip and the protagonist does not want the piano-tuner to stay with her. She prefers to encounter her husband alone. At first he hesitates but then allows the claim and leaves the room. If he would have been a man with clearly defined masculine qualities, he would have stayed with her from the beginning trying to defeat the masculine evil husband.

Besides, his blindness supports his incompetence of overpowering the husband of which the husband impudently takes advantage of. He mocks him in that he says: "[...] leave the boy; I shall deal with him later, utilising a less exalted instrument than the one with which I do my wife the honour of her immolation, for do not fear

---

[57] ibid.
[58] ibid p. 135.
[59] Hoeveler, Diana Long: *Gothic Feminism. The Professionalization of Gender from Charlotte Smith to the Brontës.* p. 6.

that in death you will be divided."[60] The husband does not see him as fully masculine because of his blindness.

4. Conclusion

The analysis of the story's characters shows that Angela Carter indeed does not focus on prescribed role models, like other gothic feminist novelists do. She does not portray the female protagonist as being solely subversive towards her husband. She is not innocent and naïve because she notices something mysterious behind him and discloses his secret: his bloody chamber containing his former wives. It is her vengeance for letting her alone for a business trip which arouses her curiosity. Therefore she changes her role of a victim into that of a perpetrator, what he actually was intending by leaving her the keys. Besides the protagonist develops her own sexuality and gains an insight into her self by being sexually aroused and recognizing that she knows at least something of pornography.

Carter depicts the husband as being evil, concealing a dark secret and being interested in sexual perverse practices. In the first place he embodies the masculine qualities but is outwitted by the protagonist's mother in the end.

The mother is the central figure in the story because she saves her daughter and defeats her husband through her male abilities. She is portrayed as a tiger-shooter; in a figurative way she shoots the tiger represented by the husband. She does not fulfil the stereotype of a woman.

As a male counterpart, the piano-tuner does not fulfil the prescribed role of a man. He is weak because of his blindness and his innocent behaviour. He is not able to defeat his opponent and is feminized through his actions.

Carter challenges sexual constructions and shows that the evil can not solely be connected with masculinity. In contrast, she demonstrates that women have the potential for being bad, as well. They are able to gain self-esteem and independence to overpower male abuse.

---

[60] Carter, Angela: The Bloody Chamber. In: *Burning your Boats. Collected Short Stories.* p. 141.

The role-making and role-breaking which Carter is following by adding gothic, feminist motifs and symbols to the story *The Bloody Chamber* can be summarized by the following quotation:

> [...] Carter's work has consistently dealt with representations of the physical abuse of women in phallocentric cultures, of women alienated from themselves within the male gaze, and conversely of women who grab their sexuality and fight back, of women troubled by and even powered by their own violence. [...] [A story] where the curiosity of the women protagonists is rewarded (rather than punished) and their sexuality is active (rather than passive or suppressed altogether.)[61]

---

[61] Makinen, Merja: "Angela Carter's The Bloody Chamber and the Decolonization of Feminine Sexuality". In: *Feminist Review* 42. pp. 3.

References

Internet sources

<http://www.megaessays.com/viewpaper/12503.html> (16/07/2007).

<http://www.dooyoo.co.uk/printed-books/the-bloody-chamber-angela-carter/1024374/> (16/07/2007).

<http://www.endicott-studio.com/rdrm/forblue3.html> (16/07/2007).

<http://www.kellscraft.com/bluebeard/bluebeard01.html> (10/01/2007).

<http://www.engl.niu.edu/kwezner/Spring%2005%20Engl%20110/Angela%20Cart er%20biography.doc> (16/7/2007).

<http://www.gradesaver.com/classicnotes/titles/bloodychamber/essay1.html> (16/7/07).

<http://www.wickedness.net/Evil/Evil%208/ozum%20paper.pdf> (16/7/07).

Article taken from a journal

Linkin, Harriet Kramer: "Telling Tales about Angela Carter". In : JSTOR. Contemporary Literature Vol. 44, No. 2. p. 340-344.

Makinen, Merja: "Angela Carter's The Bloody Chamber and the Decolonization of Feminine Sexuality". In: *Feminist Review* 42 (autumn 1992):. p. 2-15.

historical primary resources and secondary literature

Atwood, Margaret: "Running with the Tiger". In: Lorna Sage (ed.): *Flesh and Mirror*. London: Vigaro 1995. p. 117-135.

Botting, Fred: *Gothic*. London: Routledge 1996.

Carter, Angela: The Bloody Chamber. In: *Burning your Boats. Collected Short Stories*. London: Vintage 1996. p. 111-143.

Carter, Angela: *Identity Constructed/Deconstructed*. Heidelberg: Universitätsverlag C. Winter 1997.

Gamble, Sarah: *Angela Carter. Writing from the frontline*. Edinburgh: Edinburgh University Press 1997.

Hoeveler, Diana Long: *Gothic Feminism. The Professionalization of Gender from Charlotte Smith to the Brontës*. Pennsylvania: The Pennsylvania State University Press 1998.

McDowell and Rosemary Pringle (ed.): *Defining Women. Social Institutions and Gender Divisions*. Cambridge: Polity Press 1994.

Sage; Lorna: *Women in the Home of Fiction. Post-war women Novelists*. London: The Macmillan Press LTD 1992.

Schumacher, Manfred: *Das Groteske und seine Gestaltung in der Gothic Novel. Untersuchungen zur Struktur und Funktion einer Ästhetischen Kategorie*. Frankfurt am Main: Lang 1990 (= Aspekte der englischen Geistes- und Kulturgeschichte, Band 21).

Spencer, Jane: *The Rise of the Woman Novelist. From Aphra Behn to Jane Austen*. Oxford: Blackwell Publishers 1986.

Lightning Source UK Ltd.
Milton Keynes UK
UKOW051324191111

182358UK00001B/46/P